Kitty Cat

Story by Annette Smith   **Illustrations by Ben Spiby**

Here is Kitty Cat.

Kitty Cat is hungry.

Here is a butterfly.

Here comes Kitty Cat.

Look at the butterfly.

Kitty Cat is hungry.

Here is a lizard.

Here comes Kitty Cat.

Look at the lizard.

Here is Fat Cat.

Here comes Kitty Cat.

Fat Cat is hungry, too.

Look at Fat Cat!

"Come here, Kitty Cat."